REF

A

AMPHIBIANS

Text: Claire Craig
Illustrations: Dr. David S. Kirshner
Consultant: Dr. David S. Kirshner

Copyright © 1996 by the National Geographic Society

First Trade Edition 2001

Published by
The National Geographic Society
John M. Fahey, Jr., President and Chief Executive Officer
Gilbert M. Grosvenor, Chairman of the Board
Nina D. Hoffman, Executive Vice President,
President of Books and School Publishing
William R. Gray, Vice President and Director, Book Division
Nancy Laties Feresten, Director of Children's Publishing
Barbara Brownell, Director of Continuities
Mark A. Caraluzzi, Vice President, Sales and Marketing
Vincent P. Ryan, Manufacturing Manager

Library of Congress Catalog Number: 96-068037

ISBN: 0-7922-3419-7

Trade Edition ISBN: 0-7922-6571-8

Produced for the National Geographic Society by Weldon Owen Pty Ltd
43 Victoria Street, McMahons Point, NSW 2060, Australia
A member of the Weldon Owen Group of Companies
Sydney • San Francisco • London

Chairman: Kevin Weldon
President: John Owen
Publisher: Sheena Coupe
Managing Editor: Ariana Klepac
Art Director: Sue Burk
Senior Designer: Mark Thacker
Designer: Regina Safro
Text Editors: Robert Coupe, Paulette Kay
Photo Researcher: Elizabeth Connolly
Production Director: Mick Bagnato
Production Manager: Simone Perryman

Film production by Mandarin Offset
Printed in Mexico

NATIONAL GEOGRAPHIC

my first pocket Guide

REPTILES
AND
AMPHIBIANS

DR. DAVID S. KIRSHNER

INTRODUCTION

There are many reptiles and amphibians (am-FIB-ee-uhnz) in North America—from tiny frogs to large crocodiles with tearing teeth. Reptiles and amphibians are vertebrates (VERT-uh-bruts), which means they have bony backbones. Birds and mammals, such as humans, are also vertebrates. They are warm-blooded and their body temperature usually remains the same. The body temperature of reptiles and amphibians, however, changes according to how hot or cold their surroundings are.

The lizards, snakes, turtles, alligators, and crocodiles in this book are reptiles. The frogs, toads, and salamanders are amphibians. Reptiles and amphibians are quite different from each other. Reptiles have dry, scaly, or leathery skin, while most amphibians have slimy skin that must be always wet. Amphibians usually lay their eggs in water. The eggs grow into tadpoles, or larvae (LAR-vee), that live in water until they become adults. Reptiles lay their hard or leathery eggs on land, and some give birth to fully formed young.

When you see reptiles and amphibians in the wild, do not disturb them. Most reptiles attack only if another animal threatens them.

HOW TO USE THIS BOOK

Each spread in this book helps you to identify one kind of reptile or amphibian. It gives you information about the animal's size, color, appearance, and behavior. You can measure the animal's length using the ruler inside the back cover. "Where To Find" has a map of North America that is shaded to show you where the creature lives. If you find a word you do not know, look it up in the Glossary on page 76.

SNAPPING TURTLE

 Snapping turtles are strong, savage biters. The largest snapper is the alligator snapping turtle. Unlike most turtles, it is unable to pull its big head completely into its shell to escape predators.

WHERE TO FIND:
Snapping turtles swim in rivers, lakes, and swamps. Sometimes they lie in the mud in shallow water.

WHAT TO LOOK FOR:

✳ SIZE
The snapping turtle ranges from 8 to 30 inches long.

✳ COLOR
It is a muddy brownish-black color.

✳ OTHER FEATURES
The shell across its belly is very small and shaped like a cross.

✳ BEHAVIOR
It often burrows in the mud, keeping only its eyes and nostrils in the open to breathe and watch for prey.

A snapping turtle rarely leaves the water.
If it does, it becomes snappy and aggressive.

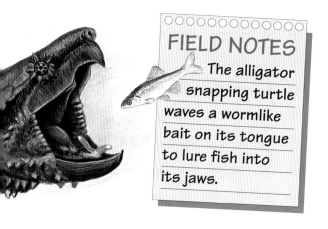

FIELD NOTES

The alligator snapping turtle waves a wormlike bait on its tongue to lure fish into its jaws.

COMMON MUSK TURTLE

 Common musk turtles release a smelly, musky fluid when they are threatened by predators. For this reason, they are often called stinkpots.

WHERE TO FIND:
Common musk turtles live in shallow, still water. You will often find them basking in high places.

WHAT TO LOOK FOR:

✳ **SIZE**
This small turtle grows between two and five inches long.

✳ **COLOR**
Its brownish-black shell is often covered with dark spots or streaks.

✳ **OTHER FEATURES**
The common musk turtle has a long neck. Its tail often has a horny tip.

✳ **BEHAVIOR**
It can climb up a slanted tree trunk to bask in the sun.

The musk turtle has stripes on its head and bristles, or barbels, on its chin and throat.

FIELD NOTES

Most turtles swim, but common musk turtles walk about on the bed of a pond or stream.

PAINTED TURTLE

The head, tail, limbs, and shell rim of a painted turtle are decorated with bright patterns. In winter, painted turtles sleep in mud at the bottom of streams, rivers, or lakes.

FIELD NOTES

A male painted turtle tries to attract a female by fluttering his long claws in front of her face.

The bright colors of this turtle make it easy to identify as a western painted turtle.

WHERE TO FIND:
Painted turtles live in waterways all across North America, from the East to the West Coast.

WHAT TO LOOK FOR:

✳ SIZE
They can grow ten inches long.

✳ COLOR
The shell is dark, usually with red or yellow markings. The head, limbs, and tail are dark, with yellow and red lines.

✳ OTHER FEATURES
Males have longer, thicker tails and longer claws than the females do.

✳ BEHAVIOR
In summer, painted turtles often bask in the sun in large numbers.

BOX TURTLE

 A box turtle can pull its head, limbs, and tail inside its tightly shutting shell to keep these soft parts safe from predators. Box turtles sometimes live for more than a hundred years.

WHERE TO FIND:
Box turtles live in dry places. In hot, dry weather they sometimes burrow into the ground to keep cool.

WHAT TO LOOK FOR:

✳ SIZE
Box turtles are four to ten inches long.

✳ COLOR
Their dark shells often have yellow or orange markings. As they grow older, box turtles can lose their bright colors and turn plain brownish black.

✳ OTHER FEATURES
If box turtles get too fat, they are unable to close their shells.

✳ BEHAVIOR
They eat plants and animals.

Male eastern box turtles, like this one, often have red eyes.

Upside-down box turtle with shell closed

SOFT-SHELLED TURTLE

 Soft-shelled turtles have soft, leathery shells. Perhaps because they are not protected by hard shells, these turtles are more aggressive than many other turtles.

WHERE TO FIND:
Soft-shelled turtles live mainly in rivers and streams. Look for a pointed snout poking out of the water.

WHAT TO LOOK FOR:

✳ SIZE
Soft-shelled turtles range between 5 and 25 inches long.

✳ COLOR
They are tan or olive, with or without darker spots, rings, or patches.

✳ OTHER FEATURES
Their hard beaks are covered by fleshy lips. Their shells look like pancakes.

✳ BEHAVIOR
Whether on land or in water, soft-shelled turtles can move quickly.

Soft-shelled turtles, like this eastern spiny softshell, are the only American turtles that have long snouts.

Soft-shelled turtles often bury themselves in the mud, with only their heads sticking out.

15

GREEN ANOLE

 The green anole (uh-NO-lee) can change color from green to brown. This tactic, called camouflage (CAM-uh-flahj), helps the lizard blend with its surroundings and hide from predators.

WHERE TO FIND:
Look for green anoles on fences, bushes, and tree trunks—and even on buildings.

WHAT TO LOOK FOR:

✳ SIZE
Green anoles grow five to eight inches long.

✳ COLOR
They can be bright green, dull brown, or any shade in between.

✳ OTHER FEATURES
They have long, pointed snouts.

✳ BEHAVIOR
The male green anole bobs its head up and down when it displays a flap of skin, called a dewlap, from its throat.

The green anole is sometimes wrongly called a chameleon (kuh-MEEL-yun)—a lizard which is well-known for changing its color.

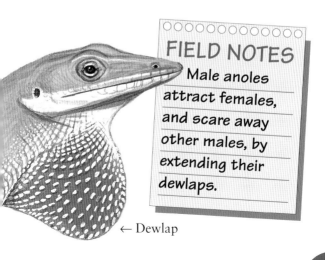

FIELD NOTES

Male anoles attract females, and scare away other males, by extending their dewlaps.

← Dewlap

COLLARED LIZARD

 Collared lizards get their name from the two black circles, like collars, around the neck of the male. Females do not always have collars. These lizards can run quickly on their back legs.

WHERE TO FIND:
Collared lizards live in hot, dry places. You may spot them perched on rocks or ledges.

WHAT TO LOOK FOR:

✱ **SIZE**
Collared lizards grow 8 to 16 inches long. Males have very large heads.

✱ **COLOR**
They can be tan, yellowish, greenish, or bluish, with dark or light spots.

✱ **OTHER FEATURES**
The male often has an orange or yellow throat or chest.

✱ **BEHAVIOR**
Collared lizards have big appetites, and often eat smaller lizards.

Male collared lizards often sit up high on rocks to view their territories.

○○○○○○○○○○○○○○○

FIELD NOTES

A collared lizard may frighten a predator away by opening its mouth to show the dark lining inside.

HORNED LIZARD

With spiny scales along the sides of their bodies, and horns on their heads, horned lizards are well armed against enemies. Some can squirt blood from their eyes at attackers.

WHERE TO FIND:
Horned lizards live mainly in grasslands and deserts. They are active on hot days, but are often hard to see.

WHAT TO LOOK FOR:

✳ SIZE
Horned lizards grow between two and a half and seven inches long.

✳ COLOR
They are mottled brown or gray.

✳ OTHER FEATURES
Horned lizards have short, blunt snouts and short, thin tails.

✳ BEHAVIOR
Horned lizards stay still until you almost step on them. Then they dart away for a short distance.

People sometimes confuse horned lizards with toads because both have fat, round bodies.

FIELD NOTES

Horned lizards eat mainly ants. They often lie quietly near ant mounds, then snatch ants as they crawl past.

SPINY LIZARD

 You have to be quick to see a spiny lizard. It is a fast and nervous creature and will often disappear swiftly behind a rock or tree trunk before you even know it is there.

WHERE TO FIND:
Look on fences, or on tree stumps. You may also find spiny lizards on the ground.

WHAT TO LOOK FOR:

✳ SIZE
Spiny lizards are between 3 and 14 inches long.

✳ COLOR
Many have bands or stripes in shades of brown, white, and red.

✳ OTHER FEATURES
They are covered in pointed scales.

✳ BEHAVIOR
Males often bob up and down to show other males the blue patches on their throats and bellies to scare them away.

The eastern fence lizard
is the spiny lizard that is
most commonly seen.

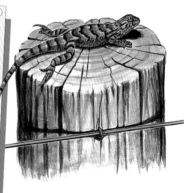

SIDE-BLOTCHED LIZARD

Side-blotched lizards are rarely shy, so you may be able to get close to identify one. The side-blotched lizard has a single dark blue or black spot on each side of its body, behind the foreleg.

FIELD NOTES

Side-blotched lizards dig their burrows near the base of bushes and rarely venture far from their homes.

Only male side-blotched lizards have the blue speckling seen here.

WHERE TO FIND:
Side-blotched lizards live on rocks or on the ground in dry areas. In warm areas, they are active all year.

WHAT TO LOOK FOR:

✳ **SIZE**
Side-blotched lizards grow four to six inches long.

✳ **COLOR**
They are brownish with lighter spots and stripes.

✳ **OTHER FEATURES**
There is often a pale stripe leading backward from each eye.

✳ **BEHAVIOR**
They can drop their tails to distract predators. They then grow new tails.

SKINK

Skinks are different from most other lizards because they have round, overlapping, fishlike scales. There are many kinds of skinks, but it is hard to tell them apart. Color and size may vary a bit.

WHERE TO FIND:
Skinks live in places with plenty of cover, such as logs and rocks—often on the edge of woodlands.

WHAT TO LOOK FOR:

☀ SIZE
Skinks range from 3 to 14 inches.

☀ COLOR
They often have brown, cream, and black stripes. Their tails can sometimes be pink, red, or blue.

☀ OTHER FEATURES
A skink can drop its tail if it is threatened by an attacker.

☀ BEHAVIOR
They smell by flicking out their tongues. The scent organs are in their mouths.

A young, five-lined skink is striped with a
blue tail. An adult loses these features.

FIELD NOTES

The bright color of
a young skink's tail
protects it because
it distracts an
enemy away from
its head.

RACERUNNER

Racerunners belong to a large group of lizards called whiptails. These sleek, fast-moving lizards have conelike heads and long, thin tails. They are agile and rarely stay still for long.

WHERE TO FIND:
You will find racerunners in open places, such as fields, sandy areas, or exposed rocks.

WHAT TO LOOK FOR:

✳ SIZE
Racerunners are usually between 6 and 11 inches long.

✳ COLOR
They are either dark, with six stripes on their bodies, or have bright green heads and seven lighter stripes.

✳ OTHER FEATURES
Males have bluish bellies and throats.

✳ BEHAVIOR
Racerunners are most active in the morning.

The blue throat of this six-lined racerunner shows that it is male.

Prairie racerunner

GLASS LIZARD

 Is it a snake, or a glass lizard? It is easy to confuse the two because both have long bodies with no legs. However, glass lizards have eyelids and earholes. Snakes do not.

WHERE TO FIND:
Glass lizards live in meadows and grasslands. Sometimes they hide under bushes and other plants.

WHAT TO LOOK FOR:

✳ SIZE
Glass lizards can grow up to 42 inches long.

✳ COLOR
They usually have black and brownish stripes. Some are speckled.

✳ OTHER FEATURES
Their tails are more than twice as long as the rest of their bodies.

✳ BEHAVIOR
Female glass lizards stay with their eggs until they hatch.

Glass lizards have hard skin, but folds along their sides make their bodies flexible.

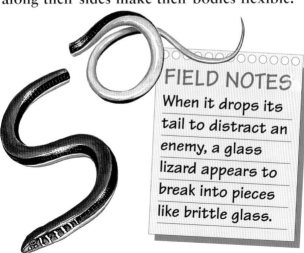

FIELD NOTES

When it drops its tail to distract an enemy, a glass lizard appears to break into pieces like brittle glass.

GILA MONSTER

Gila monsters are large, venomous lizards. They inject venom, or poison, into their prey by chewing it with their grooved teeth. They then swallow their victim whole.

The gila monster is one of only two venomous lizards in the world.

WHERE TO FIND:

Gila monsters live in deserts and open woodlands. They dig burrows, but also use those of other animals.

WHAT TO LOOK FOR:

✳ SIZE
Gila monsters are 10 to 20 inches long.

✳ COLOR
They are black with spots, bands, or patterns of yellow, pink, or orange.

✳ OTHER FEATURES
They have long, tube-shaped bodies and short limbs. They are good climbers but are usually found on the ground.

✳ BEHAVIOR
They smell with their tongues. The scent organs are in the roofs of their mouths.

GREEN SNAKE

There are two kinds of green snakes. One of them, the rough green snake, has rough, or keeled, scales. The other kind is called the smooth green snake, because its scales are smooth.

WHERE TO FIND:
Rough green snakes like to climb in shrubs or bushes. Smooth green snakes stay on the ground.

WHAT TO LOOK FOR:

∗ SIZE
Green snakes are 14 to 40 inches long.

∗ COLOR
They are bright green above and white to yellow-green below.

∗ OTHER FEATURES
Green snakes eat mainly insects and spiders. They lay long, oval eggs.

∗ BEHAVIOR
Rough green snakes are good swimmers. If they are frightened, they may dive into the water.

A smooth green snake looks shinier than a rough green snake.

Rough green snake

35

RAT SNAKE

There are many kinds of rat snakes, but they all eat mainly rodents. All rat snakes are constrictors. This means they wrap themselves around their prey and squeeze it to death.

FIELD NOTES

Rat snakes are excellent climbers. They can scale up tree trunks using only the bark to grip onto.

Yellow rat snake

WHERE TO FIND:

Rat snakes live in wooded and rocky areas. You can sometimes find them in swamplands.

WHAT TO LOOK FOR:

✳ **SIZE**

Rat snakes grow between 30 and 95 inches long.

✳ **COLOR**

Rat snakes can be yellow, orange, red, green, brown, gray, or black. Usually, they have dark stripes or patches.

✳ **OTHER FEATURES**

The young have spots or patches.

✳ **BEHAVIOR**

When rat snakes vibrate their tails in dry grass, they sound like rattlesnakes.

The red rat snake is also known as the corn snake.

KING SNAKE AND MILK SNAKE

 These snakes are not venomous. Milk snakes look dangerous because their colors are bright—a warning sign that a snake is poisonous.

WHERE TO FIND:
King snakes and milk snakes live wherever there are logs, rocks, or clumps of plants to shelter under.

WHAT TO LOOK FOR:

✳ SIZE
King snakes can reach seven feet long. Milk snakes are smaller.

✳ COLOR
King snakes are brown or black, with paler lines or speckles. Milk snakes have brown or red patches with black borders, and white or yellow in between.

✳ OTHER FEATURES
These snakes have smooth scales.

✳ BEHAVIOR
They often vibrate their tails if alarmed.

This California king snake has bands, but some California king snakes have stripes like the ones on garter snakes.

Coral snake

Milk snake

PINE, BULL, AND GOPHER SNAKE

 These three snakes are closely related. Pine snakes often live in pine forests, gopher snakes eat gophers, and bull snakes are big and bold, like a bull.

WHERE TO FIND:
Pine snakes live in the East; bull snakes in the Midwest and West; gopher snakes on the West Coast.

WHAT TO LOOK FOR:

✳ **SIZE**
These large, powerful snakes can be between three and nine feet long.

✳ **COLOR**
These snakes are white, yellow, tan, or gray. Darker patches are reddish brown to black. Occasionally, they are striped or solid black.

✳ **OTHER FEATURES**
They have small heads for their size.

✳ **BEHAVIOR**
They all feed mainly on mammals.

A gopher snake coils and
prepares to attack a predator.

RINGNECK SNAKE

The necks of ringneck snakes are often ringed with yellow or orange. To avoid being eaten by predators, some ringneck snakes release smelly fluids. Others pretend to be dead.

WHERE TO FIND:
Ringneck snakes live in moist, wooded, or open countryside across much of North America.

WHAT TO LOOK FOR:

✳ SIZE
They are 10 to 25 inches long.

✳ COLOR
Their backs are gray, brown, or black. Their bellies are yellow to red, or yellow with red toward the tails.

✳ OTHER FEATURES
Ringneck snakes are the smallest snakes mentioned in this book.

✳ BEHAVIOR
They often come into gardens around houses that are near wooded areas.

Some ringneck
snakes coil their
tails and startle attackers with a flash
of the brightly colored underside.

FIELD NOTES

Ringneck snakes
spend most of
their time under
rocks or pieces of
rotting wood.

GARTER SNAKE

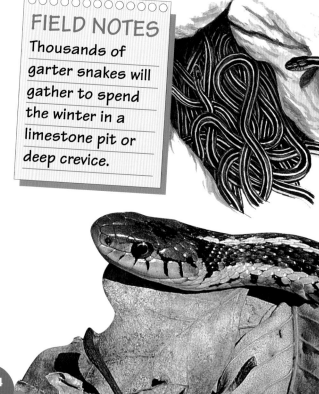

Many people keep garter snakes as pets. They rarely bite humans and feed mainly on worms, fish, and amphibians. They give birth to live young instead of laying eggs.

FIELD NOTES

Thousands of garter snakes will gather to spend the winter in a limestone pit or deep crevice.

WHERE TO FIND:
Garter snakes live anywhere from grasslands to woodlands, but they are usually near water.

WHAT TO LOOK FOR:

✳ SIZE
Garter snakes grow up to 50 inches long.

✳ COLOR
They are usually dark, with two or three light stripes. Some have no stripes.

✳ OTHER FEATURES
In the wild, a garter snake's stripes blend into the background.

✳ BEHAVIOR
If you handle a wild garter snake, it may release a smelly fluid that is meant to frighten off enemies.

A garter snake's coloring is usually a pattern of yellow, cream, or orange stripes on a dark background.

WATER SNAKE

There are many kinds of water snakes. All are excellent swimmers and can stay underwater for a long time. They have keeled, or rough, scales and give birth to live young.

Diamondback

Brown

Northern

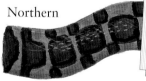

Red-bellied

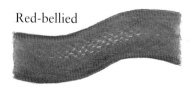

FIELD NOTES
Water snakes have many different colors and patterns. Here are just a few of them.

WHAT TO LOOK FOR:

✳ SIZE
They are 20 to 71 inches long.

✳ COLOR
Young water snakes can be plain red, green, or brown, or they can have patterns. Older adults are often dull-colored.

✳ OTHER FEATURES
They have heavy bodies and thin tails.

✳ BEHAVIOR
If a water snake is cornered or caught, it will bite and release a foul smell.

People often mistake water snakes for venomous water moccasins.

HOGNOSE SNAKE

 A hognose snake uses its shovel-like snout to dig up toads and frogs from their burrows. In defense, the victim may inflate itself with air. Then the snake will puncture it with special large teeth.

WHERE TO FIND:
Hognose snakes live in dry, sandy areas in much of eastern and midwestern North America.

WHAT TO LOOK FOR:

✳ SIZE
They are 14 to 45 inches long.

✳ COLOR
They are yellow, reddish brown, gray, or olive green, usually with darker spots. Sometimes they are solid black.

✳ OTHER FEATURES
They have short, heavy bodies with wide, flat heads and necks.

✳ BEHAVIOR
They are most active in the morning and evening because midday is very hot.

If in danger, a hognose snake may hiss and spread its neck to make itself look bigger.

FIELD NOTES

When frightened, a hognose snake may also play dead. It lies on its back with its mouth wide open.

RATTLESNAKE

When they are disturbed, rattlesnakes vibrate the rattles on their tails loudly. But they are quiet when hunting, and they strike rodents or birds swiftly and inject poison with their long fangs.

WHERE TO FIND:
Rattlesnakes live in many places, from deserts or dry grasslands to forests, and even wetlands.

WHAT TO LOOK FOR:

✳ SIZE
They are 15 to 90 inches long.

✳ COLOR
They are usually tan, gray, yellowish, or reddish, with darker patches, diamonds, or bands.

✳ OTHER FEATURES
Rattlesnakes have thick bodies, blunt, rounded heads, and slender necks.

✳ BEHAVIOR
With their heat-sensing pits in their face, they find prey in the dark.

Rattlesnakes use their rattles to warn larger animals—including humans—that they are nearby.

FIELD NOTES
A young rattlesnake's tail has one knob. A new section is added each time the snake sheds its skin.

ALLIGATOR

American alligators have broad snouts, heavy heads, and raised scales along their backs. In some areas, alligators dig ponds to make sure there is open water during the dry season.

WHERE TO FIND:
American alligators live in freshwater wetlands in the warm southeast parts of the United States.

WHAT TO LOOK FOR:

✳ SIZE
American alligators can grow over 16 feet long, but are usually smaller.

✳ COLOR
Adult American alligators are usually black with lighter bellies.

✳ OTHER FEATURES
An alligator has a second set of eyelids that acts like goggles underwater.

✳ BEHAVIOR
Adults bellow loudly during the breeding season, to attract a mate.

The jawline of an alligator seems to give the reptile a permanent smile.

CROCODILE

American crocodiles are much rarer than American alligators. Crocodiles have scaly skin, long snouts, and large, powerful tails that propel them through the water.

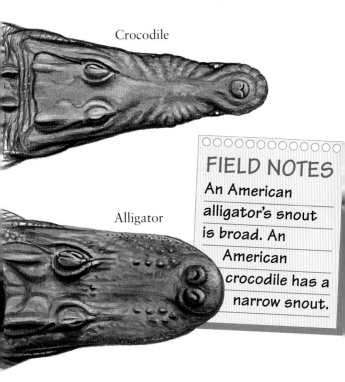

Crocodile

Alligator

FIELD NOTES

An American alligator's snout is broad. An American crocodile has a narrow snout.

WHERE TO FIND:
American crocodiles live in lagoons and mangrove swamps in southern Florida and the Florida Keys.

WHAT TO LOOK FOR:

✳ SIZE
Crocodiles can be over 16 feet long.

✳ COLOR
Adults are brownish gray to olive. The young are lighter with darker markings.

✳ OTHER FEATURES
Like the alligator, the American crocodile has a second set of eyelids.

✳ BEHAVIOR
Crocodiles are sometimes noisy, but not as noisy as alligators.

Unlike alligators, American crocodiles usually live in salty water.

MUD PUPPY

 The mud puppy is a kind of amphibian called a salamander. Most salamanders hatch in water yet spend their adult lives on land. The mud puppy, however, never leaves the water.

WHERE TO FIND:
Mud puppies live in ponds, lakes, streams, and rivers, but their dark shapes are hard to see in the water.

WHAT TO LOOK FOR:

✳ **SIZE**
A mud puppy is 8 to 16 inches long.

✳ **COLOR**
Mud puppies are gray, brown, or black. Most have dark spots.

✳ **OTHER FEATURES**
They have long, slimy bodies and paddle-shaped tails that help them to swim.

✳ **BEHAVIOR**
A female mud puppy lays up to 190 eggs. She sticks these eggs onto rocks or logs and guards them until they hatch.

The mud puppy is also known as the waterdog. It is called these names because people once thought the animal could bark.

FIELD NOTES
In warm, muddy water mud puppies have bushy, red gills. In clear, cool water the gills look smaller.

TIGER SALAMANDER

 Tiger salamanders belong to a group called mole salamanders because they dig burrows like moles do. Some have yellow and black stripes, like a tiger.

WHERE TO FIND:
Adults live underground or under rocks or logs. In spring, larvae and mating adults live in ponds.

WHAT TO LOOK FOR:

✴ SIZE
They are 6 to 13 inches long.

✴ COLOR
Tiger salamanders are usually dark, with lighter spots or stripes. Some are brownish with darker spots.

✴ OTHER FEATURES
They have riblike grooves along the sides of their bodies.

✴ BEHAVIOR
They eat most other animals that are small enough for them to swallow.

The tiger salamander is one of the
largest salamanders that lives on land.

FIELD NOTES
Young tiger
salamanders look
like axolotls
(ACK-suh-LOT-ulz)—
salamanders often
kept as pets.

EASTERN NEWT

A newt, which is a kind of salamander, starts its life in water. The adult eastern newt also lives mainly in water, but it may spend several years on land before it becomes an adult.

WHERE TO FIND:
Adult newts live in ditches, ponds, and lakes. Some young newts also live on the shady forest floor.

WHAT TO LOOK FOR:

✳ SIZE
The eastern newt is two to five and a half inches long.

✳ COLOR
It is olive-green with a yellow belly. Some newts have red spots or stripes.

✳ OTHER FEATURES
It is lizardlike in shape with a blunt, rounded head and a flattened tail.

✳ BEHAVIOR
Newts eat worms, slugs, insects, and crustaceans (crus-TAY-shunz).

Newts are less slimy than other salamanders, and have rougher skin.

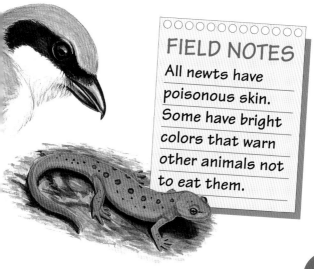

All newts have poisonous skin. Some have bright colors that warn other animals not to eat them.

RED SALAMANDER

 The red salamander belongs to the largest group of salamanders—those without lungs. These creatures breathe through their skin and the lining of their mouths They must live in moist places.

WHERE TO FIND:
Red salamanders live under rocks, rotten logs, or moss, either near or in cool, clear streams.

WHAT TO LOOK FOR:

✳ SIZE
Red salamanders are four to seven inches long.

✳ COLOR
They are red or reddish-orange with dark spots.

✳ OTHER FEATURES
They have riblike grooves along the sides of their bodies.

✳ BEHAVIOR
Earthworms are the red salamander's favorite food.

The red salamander looks like a poisonous, red eastern newt, so animals will not eat it.

If an attacker bites off a salamander's limb, the limb will eventually grow back again.

Two-lined salamander

SPADEFOOT

Spadefoots are amphibians that burrow deep into the ground in dry areas. They live underground during the day to stay moist, and come out at night to hunt for food, such as insects, and to mate.

WHERE TO FIND:
Spadefoots live in sandy or loose soil, from grasslands to deserts. Look for them during and after rain.

WHAT TO LOOK FOR:

✳ SIZE
Spadefoots are one and a half to three and a half inches long.

✳ COLOR
They are usually mottled gray, brown, or green.

✳ OTHER FEATURES
A spadefoot can develop from egg to young spadefoot in just two weeks.

✳ BEHAVIOR
Female spadefoots lay their eggs around plants in the water.

Spadefoots look like toads, but they have smoother skin and catlike eyes.

FIELD NOTES

A spadefoot has a spadelike growth on each back foot for digging. As it digs, it sinks slowly backward.

NARROWMOUTH FROG

 Some narrowmouth frogs live in burrows. The Great Plains narrowmouth frog often shares the burrows of animals such as lizards, moles, or large spiders.

WHERE TO FIND:
You are most likely to find narrowmouth frogs near water, under rocks and logs, or among leaves.

WHAT TO LOOK FOR:

✳ SIZE
Narrowmouth frogs are only one to one and a half inches long.

✳ COLOR
They vary in color. The eastern narrowmouth is brown, red, or gray.

✳ OTHER FEATURES
A male narrowmouth frog's throat is darker than a female's.

✳ BEHAVIOR
Frogs usually hop, but narrowmouth frogs often run. They eat ants.

Like all narrowmouth frogs, the eastern narrowmouth frog has a small, pointed head.

Great Plains narrowmouth frog

000000000000
FIELD NOTES
A narrowmouth frog uses a fold of skin over the back of its head to wipe insects off its eyes.

TOAD

 There are many kinds of North American toads. They are all fat and round and have short legs and dry, warty skin. They have large glands behind their eyes that produce poison.

WHERE TO FIND:
Toads live on land, but breed in water. You are most likely to find them on land on warm or rainy nights.

WHAT TO LOOK FOR:

✳ SIZE
Toads are two to seven inches long.

✳ COLOR
They are mottled brown or gray, often with darker spots.

✳ OTHER FEATURES
A toad digs burrows using the two spadelike growths on each back foot.

✳ BEHAVIOR
Many toads inflate themselves with air if they are caught. This makes it hard for predators to swallow them.

The toad, like some frogs, has a pouch of skin, called a vocal sac, under its mouth. This fills with air and helps it to croak loudly.

PICKEREL AND LEOPARD FROGS

 Pickerel and leopard frogs are closely related and look like each other. They are all spotted with two light-colored ridges running down their backs.

WHERE TO FIND:
Pickerel and leopard frogs usually live in or around water, and come out at night to feed.

WHAT TO LOOK FOR:

✳ SIZE
They are two to five inches long.

✳ COLOR
They are green or brown with darker spots, like a leopard. These spots form bands on their back legs.

✳ OTHER FEATURES
Pickerel and leopard frogs have long back limbs and slightly pointed snouts.

✳ BEHAVIOR
In summer, they may wander far from water, looking for food or new homes.

The pickerel and leopard frog look alike, but the leopard frog (above) has rounder spots than the pickerel frog (below) which has squarer spots.

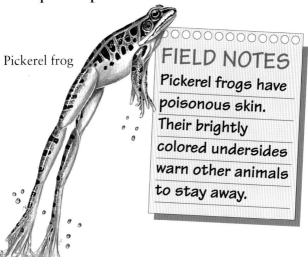

Pickerel frog

FIELD NOTES

Pickerel frogs have poisonous skin. Their brightly colored undersides warn other animals to stay away.

BULLFROG

 The bullfrog is the largest frog in North America. It lives in water and has webbed toes on its back feet. It has a well-known, deep call that sounds like *jug-o-rum*.

WHERE TO FIND:
Bullfrogs hunt for food among plants at the edge of water. Look for them in or near ponds or ditches.

WHAT TO LOOK FOR:

✳ **SIZE**
Bullfrogs grow to eight inches long.

✳ **COLOR**
They are greenish or brownish. Some have gray or brown netlike patterns on their backs and legs.

✳ **OTHER FEATURES**
Their smooth backs have no ridges.

✳ **BEHAVIOR**
Bullfrogs will eat most other animals that are smaller than themselves, including other frogs.

Male bullfrogs, such as this one, have huge eardrums behind their eyes, for sharp hearing. The females have smaller eardrums.

FIELD NOTES
Bullfrogs are noisy. You can hear a chorus of croaking bullfrogs up to a quarter of a mile away.

CHORUS FROG

 Chorus frogs are often heard but rarely seen. They gather in large numbers and call out *creeeek*, which sounds like a fingernail being dragged over the teeth of a comb.

WHERE TO FIND:
If you are lucky, you may catch sight of a chorus frog near a pond or swamp during spring.

WHAT TO LOOK FOR:

✳ SIZE
Chorus frogs are only three-quarters of an inch to one and a half inches long.

✳ COLOR
They are brownish with two or three darker stripes or rows of spots down their backs.

✳ OTHER FEATURES
Most have small, rounded toe tips.

✳ BEHAVIOR
Chorus frogs stop calling and run for cover if you come too close to them.

Chorus frogs can call loudly, despite their tiny size, because they have huge vocal sacs.

GLOSSARY

Aggressive Bad-tempered and ready to attack.

Barbel Beardlike threads on a turtle's throat that sometimes help it to feel things.

Bask When an animal lies in the sun to soak up the warmth it needs to move around.

Camouflage An animal's coloring that helps it to hide from predators by blending in with the color of its surroundings.

Crevice A small crack in a rock.

Crustaceans Hard-shelled creatures, such as crabs or crayfish, that usually live in water.

Fangs The long, hollow, or grooved teeth of a poisonous creature that it uses to inject venom into its prey.

Gills The part of the body used for breathing by creatures that live underwater.

Gland A part of the body that makes a special substance, such as venom, for the body to use.

Heat-sensing pit Tiny hollows in the skin of some snakes that can sense heat in the air, such as the heat from their prey's body.

Inflate To swell up with air.

Mate An adult animal's male or female partner with which it produces young.

Predator Any creature that hunts other creatures for food.

Prey Any creature hunted by other creatures for food.

Scent organ A part of the body that picks up smells from the air.

Territory The place where an animal lives, in which it feels safe, and which it defends.

Toe pad Pads underneath some creatures' toes that help the creature to grip onto slippery surfaces.

Venom The poisonous liquid that some animals, such as snakes, inject into their prey when they bite.

Water moccasin A kind of poisonous snake that lives around water.

INDEX OF
REPTILES

PHOTOGRAPHIC CREDITS

FIELD NOTES

FIELD NOTES

SKETCHES

FIELD NOTES

SKETCHES

FIELD NOTES

FIELD NOTES

SKETCHES

FIELD NOTES

SKETCHES

FIELD NOTES

SKETCHES

FIELD NOTES

SKETCHES

FIELD NOTES